The Heart Knows No Fear

The Heart Knows No Fear

Roopa Kamath

Highbrow Scribes Publications
New Delhi

Published 2023 by Highbrow Scribes Publications
Printed in New Delhi, India

ISBN: 978-81-956557-2-4

Note © Roopa Kamath
Forward by Amitabh Shrivastava
Illustrations by Rohit Bhasi

Typeset in Book Antiqua 11

Highbrow Scribes Publications's mission is to foster a universal passion for reading by partnering with authors to help create stories and communicate ideas that inform, entertain, and inspire, and to connect them with readers evrywhere.

Highbrow Scribes Publications books are printed on acid-free paper.

www.highbrowscribes.com

To my children Mahima and Maher,
because you are... I am!

Contents

LIGHT

"Doing as others told me, I was Blind.
Coming when others called me, I was Lost.
Then I left everyone, myself as well.
Then I found Everyone, Myself as well."

~ Rumi

Poet's Note

William Wordsworth defined poetry as 'the spontaneous overflow of powerful feeling: it originates from emotions recollected in tranquillity'. While I agree with the spontaneous overflow of powerful feelings, I don't know if it originated from emotions recollected in tranquillity because my life has been a constant search for tranquillity.

As human beings, irrespective of background, we experience the same feelings of happiness, grief, need for love and acceptance, fear, and such. We are the same pages behind different book covers, some fancy, some mundane, some hardbound, and some paperback. Yet each of us looks for love and acceptance. To be read, understood, and accepted for what and who we are.

Growing up as the youngest child in a middle-class family in Bengaluru in the 90s was an adventure. Expressing oneself had its limitations. While some topics were taboo for open discussions, others were hush-hush behind closed doors. My poetry was the only place where I could pour my emotions and feelings. They were my stress busters, my psychologist, and my friend. They didn't judge me, and I felt light after the outburst, ready to face the new day's challenges.

"Trees are poems the earth writes upon the sky, We fell them down and turn them into paper, That we may record our emptiness." – *Says Khalil Gibran*

The Heart Knows No Fear will take you on a journey that spans my childhood, teenage, early twenties and the present-day Me. The people that you feel you cannot live without, the love that makes you believe that your life will end if not for them, the experiences that only makes you stronger and takes you to where you ought to be than where you want to be, fill these pages. Words are strung like pearls on a string to make it into a necklace I adorn bravely today. An invisible thread connects me to these people and experiences, and to break them to merge into the more incredible soul is my onward journey now.

I have learned not to take myself so seriously as I have grown older. We have come here, on this plane, to learn and understand our lessons, and the soul family around us are helping us to achieve that by creating good and bad experiences to teach us and prepare us to move to the next level. Forgiveness comes easy, and life, though not easy, becomes liveable as we move towards the divine.

As George Herbert says in his poem The Pulley;
Yet let him keep the rest,
But keep them with repining restlessness;
Let him be rich and weary, that at least,
If goodness lead him not, yet weariness
May toss him to my breast.

Foreword

"I can be changed by what happens to me. But I refuse to be reduced by it."
—Maya Angelou

Poetry is a window to the soul that can evoke the deepest emotions and touch the most profound parts of our being. It is a form of artistic expression that allows us to explore the many facets of our human experience, from joy and wonder to pain and sorrow. In this beautiful collection of poems titled 'The Heart Knows No Fear', Ms. Roopa Kamath takes us on a journey through the depths of her soul, exploring the themes of Life, Light & Love. Each poem is a unique expression of the author's varied emotions and experiences, capturing the beauty and complexity of human nature and sensibilities.

The poet's journey is often a solitary one, a search for meaning and purpose that can take us to the edges of our consciousness. Yet, through their work, they can connect us with a shared humanity, and in doing so, offer us a glimpse of the universal truths that unite us all.

These poems by Roopa on Life, Light & Love are an invitation to join her on this journey. Her collection of poems offers a rich tapestry of emotions, images, and ideas that will resonate with readers of all ages and backgrounds. They are a celebration of the beauty and complexity of life, and a reminder of the power of love to heal and transform.

Love is the most profound emotion we can experience as human beings, and it is the foundation of our existence. As the famous poet Rumi once said, "Love is the bridge between you and everything." The poems on 'love' capture the essence of this powerful emotion, delving into its many facets and complexities, from the joy and excitement of falling in love to the pain and heartache of losing it.

Life is the thread that binds us all together, and it is the focus of many of the author's poems. Life is a journey, full of twists and turns, ups and downs, and Ms. Kamath's words remind us to savour every moment, to embrace the challenges and the joys, and to live life to the fullest.

Life is the thread that binds us all together, and it is the focus of many of the author's poems. Life is a journey, full of twists and turns, ups and downs, and Ms. Kamath's words remind us to savour every moment, to embrace the challenges and the joys, and to live life to the fullest.

Finally, Light is another theme that is explored in the second chapter of this collection, symbolizing hope, inspiration, and the search for truth. As the great writer Victor Hugo once said, "To love beauty is to see light." Roopa's poems on light shine a beacon of hope and optimism, illuminating the path ahead and inspiring us to keep moving forward, even in the face of adversity.

The writing style of Roopa is truly captivating and distinctive, bringing her poems to life with an evocative and lyrical quality. Her use of imagery, metaphor, and language is masterful, conveying emotions and ideas with depth and richness.

It is imbued with a sense of honesty and vulnerability that is both refreshing and relatable. She speaks from the heart, unafraid to explore her own experiences and emotions, and in doing so, connects with readers on a deep and personal level.

One of the most striking aspects of Roopa's writing style is her ability to seamlessly blend different poetic forms. She effortlessly shifts between different styles and structures, creating a dynamic and engaging reading experience that keeps readers enthralled.

Her Author's Note speaks about the power of poetry as a means of self-expression and emotional release. In a world where it can be challenging to express oneself openly, poetry provides a safe and nurturing space to explore our deepest thoughts and feelings. Roopa's poems are a testament to the power of poetry as a form of self-discovery and healing.

So, sit back, relax, and immerse yourself in this beautiful collection of poems. Let this inspire you to embrace your journey with courage, grace, and passion.

AMITABH SRIVASTAVA

Senior Alumni NSD,
Actor & Sangeet Natak Akademi Awardee
March 2023, Delhi.

LIFE

"When I went to school, they asked me what I wanted to be when I grew up. I wrote down "Happy". They told me I didn't understand the assignment and I told them they didn't understand life."

- John Lennon

The Truth

The clouds move away, revealing the sun
Like truth which cannot be hidden behind any garb,
Like the love that cannot be disguised under any pretense,
Like tears that cannot hide behind false laughter.

A question and an answer
Will it make any difference?
Can it change anything?
What happened cannot be reversed.

Like the lovelorn Meera; Seeking her beloved.
I search the whole world where art thou?

Memories as waves crash through my consciousness,
Laughter like chariots rides in all splendour.
Promises and vows echo in my head,
But then the clouds move away, revealing the sun.

Journey

Like the dark clouds that shower and pass,
Like a storm that destroys and vanishes.
The dark phases of life grind and move on,
The heartbreaks and aches crush and disappear.

Without turning back, they move on.
For if they do, they will be destroyed too.
Under the showers now grows a beautiful garden,
The storm clears the unwanted for newer life to emerge.

Dark phases enhance the silver lining of the cloud,
Heartbreaks strengthen the phoenix spirit.
No finality do I see in life, Like a stream, it flows.

Gathering experiences till it meets the sea,
Like my soul that is on its journey to the almighty.

I Am Not Alone

Walking in the dark woods
Tiny glow worms sparkle in all splendour
The wildflowers bloom to the fullest
Euphoric fragrance and blissful light show me the way.

The sun and the rain take turns
Shadowing me like an umbrella
Under the golden glow, my skin basks
Under the gentle shower, my heart rejoices.

The moon and the stars play silent music
And the Earth dances with me
The breeze embraces me tenderly
Tiny shrubs and trees form my constant companions.

Lilting voices of my children
The constant call from my partner
And reassurance from my friends
Asserts that I am not and never will be alone.

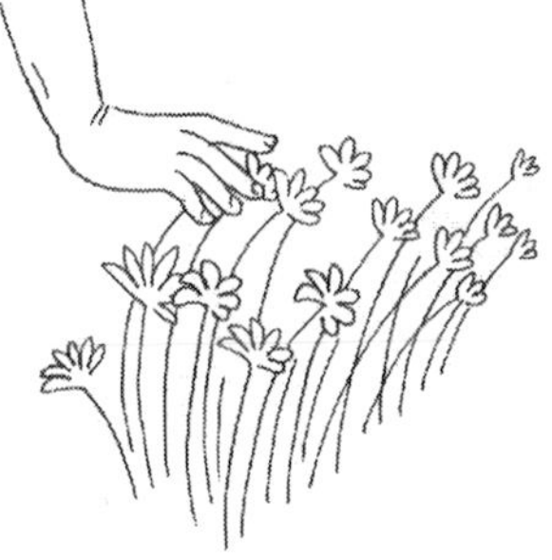

Death

The moon shines in the dark of the night
Stealing unhappy glances at me.
The breeze silently makes its way
Gently carrying my tears away.
The creatures of the night have turned silent
Mourning my death with me.

The Heart Knows No Fear

The heart knows no fear,
The uncertain fog of the future has cleared,
No apprehensive nights worrying about untold incidents,
I am free from my fears and my happiness.
A calm spreads its warm hands across my being,
Nurturing the raw wounds and my wounded soul,
I refuse to be sad or happy,
I just want to be me.
I want to set my soul free from the cages of emotions and
feelings.
The warmth of the body,
The tenderness of a hand I can't feel,
The honeyed words of love,
The accusing cruel phrases I can't hear,
The soul refuses to gel with another,
Soulmates touch and go, an unfulfilled trial,
The lips refuse to twirl into a frown,
The eye refuses to shed pearls of tears,
The heart refuses to heave and sigh in pain,
They have seen the trials of life test me time and again.
A noble being resides inside the hollow of my body,
A soul that is pious as anybody's.
Constant insults hurled, suspicions surface,
The dew on a lotus petal untouched remains,
Am I unworthy of your love?
Or you of mine?

I refuse to belong to your land of love;
Where gigantic shadows of untruth loom large on a tiny
truth,
Where assumptions and insecurities shake the root of trust,
Where love needs proof of undying commitment and
loyalty,
I refuse to belong to that land of yours.
My self-esteem refuses to be crushed and powdered,
By the ego of your so-called love,
I refuse to be anything but me.

Who Am I

I am the vast expanse of the wide blue sky,
I am the ray of trickling sunlight amidst cottony white clouds,
I am the bird that soars high, knowing it will never touch the sky,
I am the busy bee gathering nectar,
I am the colourful flowers spread across green meadows,
I am the sweet nectar that connects them both.

I am the mother that suckles the child,
I am the child that entwines with the mother,
I am the peace and the sustainer,
I am death and the destroyer,
I am the created and the creator,
I am the needy and the giver.

I am the bright sunlit day,
And the cold, moonless night,
I am the lover and the beloved,
I am the sinner and the sinned,
I am the killer and the killed,
I am the id, the ego, and the free spirit.

I am me, as in every you,
I am the freedom that throbs in the hearts of every caged soul,
I am the soul of the entire world.
That lives in every you and me.

True Self

A silence that pierces my heart and head,
Tears well up in my eye,
Where has my true self gone?
The laughter has died down.
And the self-esteem drowned.
The light that danced in my eyes has switched off,
The lilt in my steps has disappeared,
The child in my heart has suddenly grown up,
The trust in another I have lost.
Strangers in the name of friends, do I see
Where has my old self gone?
Finding and sharing joy in little things,
Bringing a smile to your lips and mine.

Where is my true self?
I can't find her anymore.
The mirror reflects someone ugly,
It cracks, knowing not what to show,
Which is the mask and the true face?
Why can't I be myself and still be loved?
'Tis a question that seems to have no answer,
Changing to the needs of everyone,
To fill the nooks and corners of their lives.

I have lost myself in the ever-changing need to change myself.

To satisfy those who refuse to be satisfied,

To overcome the faults that are not my own,

To clear my name of the thousand names that I have been given,

The witches were burnt and are gone now.

But in the eternal fire of love, I burn and still can't find myself,

Bold and strong that they were; they have died a courageous death,

Weak and meek, I see myself dying a torturous death every day.

The Waiting

The waiting never stops for things that never will come,
The eye doesn't rest till it scans every nook and corner,
The ear picking the slightest sound, turns to a blind wall each time,
The heart survives, cause the wait never ends.

Friends who may never return,
For events that may never unfold,
For conversations that may never take place,
For destiny sometimes disagrees with free will.

Is it the unattainable that the heart desires,
Knowing the pain of separation that opens the flood of words.
Once the desire is fulfilled, there will be a desert of silence,
Until the pain in expectation and disappointment rises in time.

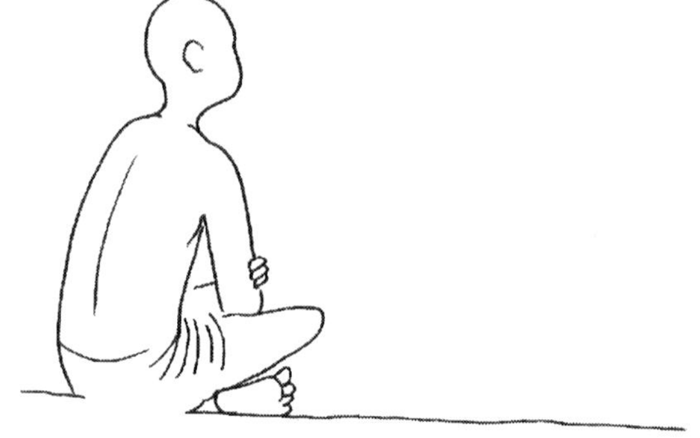

Spring

The ticking of the clock echoes in the night,
The silent grasshopper moves on.
A dragonfly leaps towards the light,
As the night gives way to the dawn.

The summer heat is cooled by showers of rain,
And the beauty of the trees kisses the eye.
And at that moment, vanishes all the momentary pain,
As I walk on the bed of mayflowers into a carpet of sighs.

Each is different from the other,
The green of the leaves and the shades below the trees.
Yet they are in natures family brothers,
With differing fragrances, they are the same breeze.

A solitary song of the merry bird singing far away,
And the blooming of the sky to face the day.
All seem to whisper in my heart and ear as if to say,
To convey, to celebrate that spring is on its way.

Our Mother

The colours that spread across the sky,
God is leisurely painting the sky.
The peaches, the beautiful blues,
And the dust of white clouds,
Are but the poetry of thoughts.

Unpredictable is nature now,
When she might lash out.
Cyclones, hurricanes, floods and earthquakes,
A disturbing thought triggers my mind,
She doesn't hear the cries of the masses.

She has turned a deaf ear,
Her eyes burning red with rage,
Her body trembles the insensitivity, unable to bear.
When all along, she has been the most forgiving mother,
why have we underestimated her might?

A mother can create or destroy,
Nurture, nourish or make us all perish.
Doomsday, Oblivion, and Judgment Day are a concept that
approach,
Concepts transforming into reality.
Nobody wants to learn any more.

They believe they have the license to kill and destroy,
But just turn around and see.
Who is having the last laugh!
A loving mother is ever ready to spank,
Her young ones to correct them to show them the right
path.

Through the untrodden path of suffering,
Which we believe can't touch us.
It is taking a slow and steady walk,
Life-ready to leave; hopefully, man learns before it's too
late.

No Man's Land

Urban lights and dark shadows,
Spread slowly into the night.
The scorpion prowls into the privacy of the elite,
Stung by it, each dies a painful and slow death.

The pavements covered by the corpses of labourers,
Mowed down by the drunk, the rich.
Bitten by bedbugs and mosquitoes,
They are immune to the calamities of everyday.

A life of pseudo-isms of pretense,
A middle-class existence.
Striving to reach above the clutches of poverty,
Yet the lights of the rich are still far away.

Under the depths of debts and unfulfilled desires,
Living each day under a
new guise of strength.
Happiness and Courage,
Where do I stand?

Neither here nor there,
Waiting for acceptance,
waiting to reciprocate.
Along with me stand the
likes of me,
In no man's land.

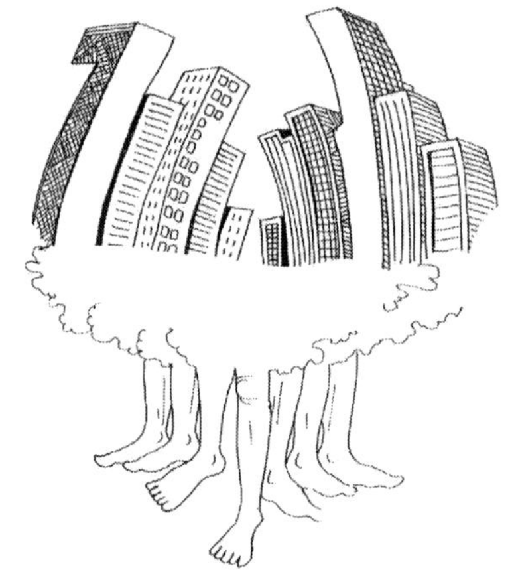

Life To Me Is

Carpet of slain hearts lush red,
A breeze of tortured sighs suffocating.
Flowers of rotten bodies reality,
Songs a dirge, silent and painful.

Life colourfully black,
Truth unwanted shadows.
Mirrors filled with darkness,
Feelings of loneliness and scary nights.

Sun, a burning ball of fire.
Friends, a mere word, pretenders,
Love, desirable yet unlovable,
Future, bright and blindingly bleak.

Relationships binding controllers.
Corporeal body, a chained bondage,
Soul a trapped bird,
Death, the only naked truth.

Because I Am Not Like Them

Untamed and wild, they call me,
Because I am not like them.
They have mastered the art of all guises,
To unlearn and undo the mask of centuries
Of culture and civilization,
Which they have carefully adorned and imbibed,
At home, with the roles that they play,
To be like me, they do not wish to be.
Glowing in the light of false glories,
Walking on a tightrope of rules and regulations,
Each trying to outdo the other, with their natural self lost,
a long time ago.

They talk of things great;
But are lost to the little pleasures.
At each crossroad, they stand an eternity,
Their soul, time and again crushed by their ruling mind,
They walk on the path of familiar deceit and falsehoods,
They drown only to emerge as a more refined and polished
person,
Then they call me untamed and wild,
Because I am not like them.

As I Walk Down Memory Lane

The dry leaves crack beneath my feet,

Fall has gone, summer is showing its heat.

Spring is on its way,

And I lie in my memory lane seeing flowers as they sway.

The sea of faces, the noise of indistinguishable voices,

Parading in front of my eyes without a choice.

A choice to see whom I wish and hear the soothing voices
of the few,

A stream flows without giving way to the dew.

I walk down memory lane smiling at some,

And sometimes, with me, somebody, my favourite song
hums,

As I walk ahead, I have my reasons to sigh.

I ask myself why my beloved ones left me in my loneliness
to cry,

I see goals I have achieved, and pride overcomes me.

And the strength I gain to laugh at the dreams unachieved,

I watch the children of yesterday as today's youngsters.

And perhaps the vision of tomorrow is a quiet blur,

I don't remember growing, when did they?

Yes, life and time wait for none,

So as to say.

Relationship

Some relationships: unclear; unfinished,
Hard to live this mundane life.
Senseless and demanding,
A disturbing silence descends on the grave reality called life.
The lights have disappeared, shadows loom,
The eyes have dried up; there is a famine for tears.
Vacuum gulps my heart and my soul,
Like a lifeless feather, I float without a sense of time or place.
Where is the sacred thread that connects us?
Let me cut it and set myself free.
Every day, a disturbed mind, a helpless soul,
Seeks answers to questions that seem unanswerable.

Where Do Feelings Go?

Looking back at my bruised heart,
And battered ego,
Nursing a relationship, a journey so tedious,
Yet a sigh of relief, I let go today.
Multiple roles and emotions; hard to comprehend,
Harder still to live,
Like the soul relieved of its body,
I float in a plane of tranquillity.
Feelings for people who don't and can't value it,
Emotions that hinder the quest for things,
Suddenly seem to vanish today,
With a smile, as I walk today, I question,
Where do feelings go?

Dreams

Under the dark blue blanket of the night,
A tiny thought is born, wanting to light up the sky,
Dreams that are dreamt with eyes wide open,
Dreams like the thoughts that want to outshine the stars.
A million reasons I find, why shouldn't I,
And a million reasons, others find for me,
Yet with a throbbing passion, it pulsates despite all odds,
Surviving the mundane calamities of every day.
Dreams that defy the ordinary, Dreams that refuse to fade out,
Hopping and skipping their way into everyday thoughts,
Fighting to live and be realized.
Like the Kite are my dreams,
I tug at the string, hoping it will soar high,
Touch the pinnacle, if there is one,
And I know, in my hand, it lies.

A Journey Has Begun

Like a serpent baring its fangs,
Each day unfolds,
My own death, I cannot predict.
Out of sheer dread, would I perish?
Or would its sweet fangs liberate me from this uncertain world,
Would it turn out to be an anaconda?
Would it slowly relish suffocating and crushing me?
Knowing fully that I have nowhere to run,
It's grasp, like a jealous lover reluctant to let go.
Is the world happy with the lessons it has taught me?
Bitter-sweet, are there more in its invisible fold.
Am I a ready learner, or do I have no choice?
The corpse of my duties heavy on my delicate shoulder,
To unburden it on the pyre, I move on with
Cracked bare feet on the thorny path.
A journey has just begun.

Tryst With The Dark

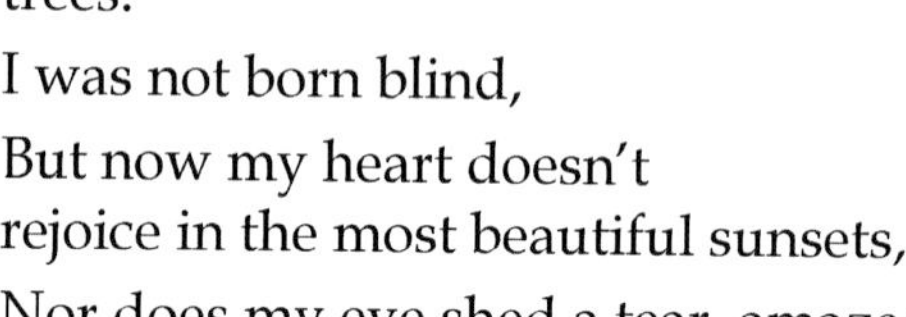

I was not born deaf,

But now I cannot hear the
pitter-patter of the rain,

Nor can I listen to the merry
song the breeze sings,

Nor of a thousand little birds
chirping behind shadowed
trees.

I was not born blind,

But now my heart doesn't
rejoice in the most beautiful sunsets,

Nor does my eye shed a tear, amazed at the crimson sky,

Nor is it overwhelmed by the endless blue of the ocean,

Looking past the joyous into the unknown,

A blind eye seems to say I was not born blind.

I was but born with a heart that throbbed and lived,

But now a dead piece of churned mass lies there,

Squeezed beyond recognition, once, which harboured a
thousand feelings,

Has it stopped beating, or is it not bothered anymore,

Yet a dead crass of meat lies unchartered n unattended.

My mind is blank as I sit in a vacuum,

Where the sense of time or place doesn't touch me,

Nor do I hear the voice or feel the warmth of anybody
around.

Am I dead to the feeling, or has my body given up,

A hopeless battle fought and left defeated; has it
withdrawn?

Surrendered to the merciless tryst with the dark.

A Young Guy And A Girl Met In A Sultry Old Town

Wild Butterflies in the outstretched garden,
Tiny Glowworms contained in silvery jars,
Persistent crickets in a symphony,
Croaking frogs to complete the picture.
A young girl and a guy met in a sultry old town,
Under a mango tree, to be bound in Holy alliance,
The picture seemed perfect,
Dreams woven into palatial cobwebs.
And then fear crept in. . .
Fear that takes over dreams and wipes it clean,
Fear that shadows the bright sunlit room,
Fear that turns a Yes into a No,
Fear that fears its own life.
Did I break your heart or my own dreams?
I cannot say,
For eerie silence has crawled into the nooks and corners of
my life.
Answers, I seek not, for I am, but a stranger,
Forgiveness is all I ask of thee to unburden a heavy soul,
A Soul that carries the picture of an optimist guy ,
With a hundred and one dreams,
The picture though smoggy, comes to life often.
Breathing life into memories frozen in time,
Hung like precious pictures in the sanctum sanctorum of
my soul.

Why Doesn't Life Let Me Be

Why doesn't life let me be?

Entangling me in its web of deception.

I cannot, from its clutches, escape.

In the name of love and affection,

Binding me to the worldly.

Surrendering to the bliss of lust,

My soul seems to question,

Why doesn't life let me be?

Why doesn't life let me be?

Into mood swings, and a roller coaster of emotions, it takes me

Erupting into a seamless volcano of thoughts and senseless words.

A silent voice screams into the deaf ears of my beloveds,

And not-so-beloveds too.

Clobbered feelings and cobwebs of memories refuse to live again

Yet life dances the mystical dance

And awakens me from my hibernation,

And I timidly question,

Why doesn't life let me be?

This Modern World

In the lifeless existence of this modern world,

Of shadowy dungeons with halogen lights,

Of programmed languages and words.

I look into your eyes to see what is in your sight,

The flesh of each creeping life and the blood draining from dried skeletons.

The suffocation of each feeling kills you softly, slowly and steadily.

The heart, now the mind, resembles calculative, scheming, planning and gluttonous.

Devouring each moment, without enjoying the pleasure of sharing,

Do I see you among them constantly?

Cowards in mass, yet bravery a facade,

Innocence lost, virgin emotions waiting to be explored and satisfied.

But what do I see? Are you with them, who the unholy pleasures seek?

No, sometimes the pleasure in such a simple word has an orgasm, in it confined.

How Do You Feel To See The End?

The gentle breeze has passed you by,
The sun has set,
The last note of the song has been sung,
The last drop of the rain has fallen.
How do you feel to see the end?

Vacuum slowly sucking you into oblivion,
Quicksand giving you no time to think or act.
A whirlpool swallowing you,
A Tornado snatching you away,
How do you feel to see the end?
Are you immune to the pain!
Does it still curdle your stomach!
Do you want to scream yourself hoarse?
Or lie numb, lifeless, in a corner?
How do you feel to see the end?
Is there any hope that you still hang on to?

Are you still waiting for your prayers to be answered?
Does your heart still lie to you?
Does your mind give you reasons to survive and go on?
How do you feel to see the end?

Depression

Endless sleep doesn't rest you enough,
Nor does any amount of medication.
When you, in a depressed state, survive,
Nothing can raise your spirits and make you feel alive.
A sense of hopelessness spreads,
A tiny fear starts gnawing its way into your soul.
The mind goes blank, refusing to acknowledge,
And the heart goes numb as the day unfolds.
Flowery smiles and a happy disposition, I carry,
A burden to my heart and soul.
When I, in solitude, unmask myself,
A crushing relief escapes the throttled spirit.

A mountainous effort to get out of bed,
Sit up at my desk and work.
Bills need to be paid, and a family needs to be fed.

Happy Birthday To Me

As another autumn of my life passes me by,
I turn to see,
The crinkled and wrinkled laugh lines,
And know,
I have lived a good life.
The silver threads that hold the memories,
Memories of pearly happy moments.
A heart that refuses to age with the body,
Making a mockery of the mortal self.
I have lived and will live on beyond you,
It seems to say.
Yes, another autumn passes by. . .
Giving way to the spring of my life.

The Urn

Raindrops like tears wash away the pain,
Imprints never there, but have visited,
For thy eyes and heart have felt the touch,
To remind us that after a dark night, the dawn blooms,
And the spring blossoms after the winter.
Red and Yellow weathered leaves float on a bed of
luminous blue,
Untouched, our soul remains through the experience and
pain,
Let's learn the lessons we have come to learn,
Enriching our souls before the breaking of the Urn.

Memory

Simmering thoughts crossing the threshold of my mind,
Memories made, yet so short-lived,
A Canvas that often erases its own art,
Blank, my mind goes, thoughts and feelings alike.

Believe me, they do not, Laugh at me; they do,
Yet, not a pretense but a gift from God,
A memory that has no memory of its own.

Each day I live as if it is new,
Each feeling I experience for the first time,
Perhaps from this whirlpool called life,
A boon to survive and rejuvenate.

The constant swamp of existence sucks me in,
Only to let go as I breathe deep within,
And everything vanishes, To place me in oblivion.

My Onward Journey

I have felt this feeling before,
A feeling of emptiness,
A sudden void in my chest,
A vacuum sucking my life out.
My head feels empty and light,
And my sight is blurred,
I stare into empty space,
Tinnitus rings in my ear.
The anchor has been lifted,
And I float aimlessly.
The Mast has no wind to direct it.
A stormy life ahead, I reckon.
In a strange time and a stranger place,
I find myself.
I am ready for my onward journey,
But the maps, in my kin's hands, lie.

Utopia

I peered through the doorway.
Into the unknown world,
Was it a door or a trap to catch my attention?
Luring me into a thought of a better world

Hopelessness and a sense of fear of this world
Pushing me into a deluded expectation.
Carefully wrapping time in a perfect gift box the
excitement of which supersedes the content.

Time passes, illusions melt and reality strikes
No doorway, no traps, nor a better world lies out there.
The wrapper unfolds, holding our tomorrow,
In this world in this time.

Why do I look outside to find the Utopia?
When each day, I can slowly build my own peering,
through the doorway of my soul,
A beautiful Reunion, I see in eternity.

Life

Diving deep into my being, He pulled out my soul,
And the souls of my children,
Juggling them, throwing care to the wind.
While he, in his melancholy, a sadistic joy derived.
While we, with masks of happiness, walked.
He put forth a face of deprivation and grief.
And they, who stood and watched,
Thought us heartless and low, How would they know?
That body with no soul hardly could conjure a heart,
Years of training didn't betray us,
And years of training didn't betray him either.
A shameless woman puts her head down in disgrace,
While a pious man walks on, his head held high.

LIGHT

'Your vision will become clear only when you can look into your heart. Who looks outside, dreams, who looks inside, awakens.'

- Carl Jung

Charanamrit

There she walks with the water that washed her beautiful feet,
She falters as her tear-filled eyes cannot see.
Her shivering hand carries a bowl for her beloved to consume,
Unwell, he lies there waiting for the drink that would revive him.

She knows that her place in hell is sealed for this offence so grave,
Yet nothing is greater to her than Krishna's life.
Seeing her beloved in pain, she dies a thousand deaths,
She knows that she might never be reunited in an earthly marriage.

For a selfless offence, she committed,
The gopikas stand at bay, watching the beautiful maiden.
As she traces her path to the bedside,
Gently lifting her beloved in her arms.

She pours the drink into his mouth,
The water of a true devotee and the washed feet of a lover.
The Charanamrit that would give him solace ,
Her teardrops mix with the water taking away all her sorrows.

Her Krishna drinks, giving her eternal celestial joy,
A mere mortal she is not, but his consort, his love.
In that moment of melancholy, realization dawns,
And all else fades away.

Radhey

In the silence of the night, a silhouette makes her way,
Into the welcoming arms of her lover.
Standing by the Yamuna, his flute beckons her each night,
Away from the mortal world into eternal bliss.

Without a second thought leaving behind her sleeping
mate,
She tiptoes into the warm embrace of her lover.
The marriage of the soul and body each night,
Passionate lovers in the silence of the night.

Untying her hair, letting the breeze devour the mane,
Apparel and ornaments adorn the ground.
The shimmering waters and the full moon bear witness to
their love,
The creatures of the night leave the lovers alone.

Alone to rejoice as they indulge in playful lovemaking,
Celestial beings shower flowers, making a soft carpet.
The breeze gathers perfume from a million flowers,
And the fireflies create a mesmerizing ambience.

Yet the lovers are oblivious to these wonders.
Celebrating their togetherness,
The lovers are but an extension of each other.
Breaking all the rules, they care a damn about the world ,

The world is trivial; nothing but their love they know.

An eternal love story for the world to remember they leave behind,

Questions that might never be answered. Feelings that might never be explored.

Reminding us to love without reason and live moments to the fullest.

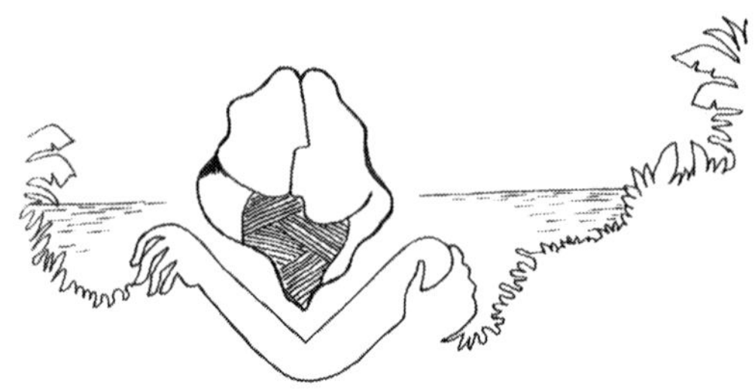

I Have Nothing To Offer You,
My Love

I have nothing to offer you, my love,
But my wrinkled hand filled with the sweetest offering of
my affection.
My hazy eyes filled with your image,
This grey hair that has lived in expectation of your arrival.
My weak limbs that have sought every nook and corner of
this world for you,
And finally found you in my heart.

A madwoman walked the length of her land singing your
praise,
The kohl of her eyes smudging as her tears trickled in pain.
Her once beautiful shiny hair now tangled with your
thoughts,
Hunger and thirst didn't touch her morose-filled body.
Age has not dampened her spirit.
Like a lamp that flickers its best; before it blows off.
Her love for you has only brightened her being,
Her penance will come true, she is sure.
Her eternal lover will come and carry her across this
world,
And she sings, blind to the mockery the world makes of
her.
With her wrinkled hands and body ripened by age,
Welcoming the eternal youth of her lord Krishna into her
soul.

Meera sings in ecstasy and says,
I have nothing to offer you, my love.

Meera

A bowl of poison turns into nectar at the very thought of
you,
A pit full of snakes turns into a garden of fresh flowers.
A fiery night with its wild tentacles calmed by a soothing
breeze,
A burning temple hushed by a shower of gentle rain.

Your magical flute spreads its alluring music,
Into each and every nerve of my troubles.
Freeing me from the charade of this existence,
In search of your love.

Childhood, youth and my life; I have lived,
Nothing beyond it, the heart of my eye wants to see.
Holding your statue, your
eternal bride stands in front of
you,
Accept me, I do not say.

Let me love and rejoice in your
name and thought,
Let my madness fill my being
and take me away from this
hollow existence.
The rules and regulations of this
world don't touch me,
Because my soul is not my own,
it has merged in your thoughts.

A crazy woman wanders in the dunes of the desert,
Scorching heat and burning sand do not touch her.
Merrily, she walks carrying her Krishna in her soul.

50

On The Banks Of Yamuna

Tangled hair that captures the wind,
Droopy eyes that haven't seen a wink of sleep,
Carelessly thrown attire uncaring for the world,
Tears that spill from melancholic dove-like eyes.

Searching wildly for her beloved,
On the banks of the Yamuna,
A silhouette moves aimlessly,
Losing sense of time, she craves for her beloved.

Calling lovingly in a whisper,
Now shouting and screaming herself hoarse,
Where are you?
Her eyes have not rested; her heart is in distress.

Can't you feel her pain?
Can't you come to her rescue? She lives in your very name.
And you in her soul and every cell of her body.

In some palatial world beside another damsel,
Where are you?
Can you not hear her, Krishna?
Radhe is calling.

Where Do I Seek Solace?

The invisible tears that wet my wrinkled face.
A bottomless pit, my heart has become,
A dark abyss with nothing to hold on to.
Where do I seek solace?

Oh Sai, give me the strength to live a solitary life,
No partners do I seek,
On my path to you, a slow journey has begun.
Hurt and humiliated at each junction.

A hope that things will change, a mirage,
Where do I seek solace?
A hundred times, this question crosses my mind,
My hands reach out and return empty.

My eyes have not found a wink of sleep,
Nor my heart a sigh of relief.
What is this existence called life?
I haven't found the answer, have you?

An insecurity that seems to spread its wings in every
corner of my life,
The pungent odour of a seemingly dead heart slowly
encompasses all.
A repulsive thought like cancer tears me apart.
Loneliness is not as fancy as it sounds,
It is like a million dreams being crushed with a single foot.

And to find the foot and set myself free, I try
But like an invisible sadist, it attacks when I least expect it
to.
Leaving me unnerved and lost,
Reviving the question, Where do I seek solace?

You Are The Means, And You Are The End

Like an endless black abyss. . .
The beginning and end, lost, engulfed by the darkness,
Your desires for materialistic things have no end,
Trying to satisfy your need has left me hopeless,
With hope, I started on this path,
Realization dawns now when all else is lost,
Craving for the human flesh you do not possess,
Nor for the selfless love that I want to bestow upon you,
Things that are here now and gone forever within a wink,
Catch the fancy of your heart and eye.
Compete with them, I cannot,
Nor catch up with the race against your indulgence.
A futile attempt to see a content smile on your face,
How do I proceed from here? Oh, Sai, help me. . .
I am like a lost ship amid a tempest, Hold my hand and
bring me ashore.
I have no one else, who will understand my plight,
Nor empathize but you.
Open your eyes and look at me, my lord,
Bless my life and take me in your fold,
Guide my soul into the ocean of your heart,
No turns do I want to take now, that I have found you.
Let my tears wash your feet, and my devotion serve you.
Your child has come to you. Oh, Sai. . .
For you are the means, and you are the end.

Radhe Shyam

And then she said, never let me go,
Hold me tight, and let us be one forever,
Let our names be entwined, a mystical smile he smiled.
The laws of the world didn't bind them, then what did?
How could their names be entwined?
A small desire of his beloved, couldn't he fulfil?
And didn't he? When we call out to him. . .
Radhe Shyam!

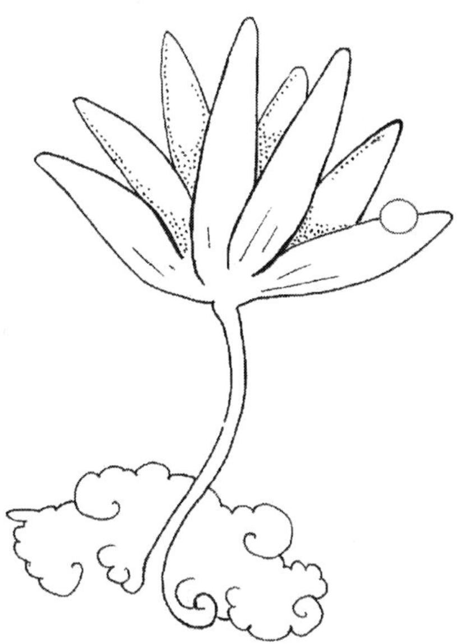

Never Let Go Of My Hand

I look up to you, my lord, and I see you smiling down at me,
Why do thy lips curl into a mystical curve,
Mysterious yet so soothingly welcome,
Cos, I know that I am safe in thy hands.
In troubled times, I extend my hands to hold yours,
Yet I see not yours,
Have you abandoned me when I need you the most?
Thoughts of blasphemy cross my mind.
Then I see you, taking me in your stride,
Guiding me gently across this ocean of painful trials,
I see you taking my hand in your invisible hold,
And I understand. . .
My hands might weaken their grip and let go,
But your loving hold will only strengthen me with time,
Guiding me and anchoring my faith in you with each passing moment.
I pray to thee, My Lord, never let go of my hand.

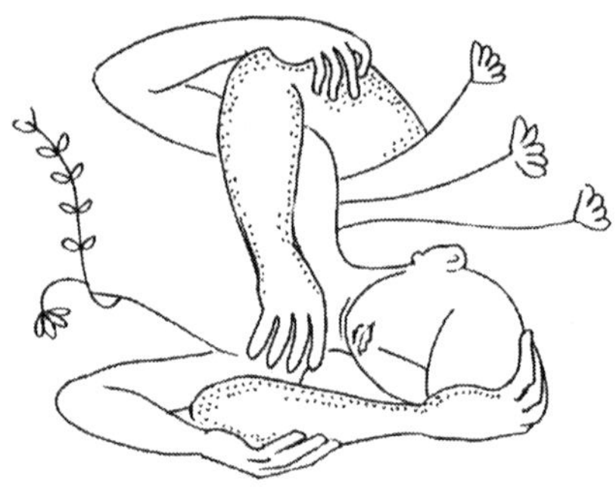

The Struggling Caterpillar

Little droplets of rainfall,
As I see you stretch your wings and take to flight.
Sadness overwhelms me as I breathe a sigh of relief.
From a little nobody struggling to hold ground,
You grew up into an ugly being with hideous designs,
Just like my soul, falling, failing, hurting and rising again,
A life that has come with its syllabus of lessons.
Need to learn mine before my time runs out,
Ugly truth and hideous realities hurt me,
Only when the curtain of illusion is removed,
Do I see how beautiful life is?
The struggling caterpillar grows to be the pupa,
Laboriously tearing itself away from the make-believe shelter,
And into the world, an amazing butterfly is born.
And I hold on and ask God,
Why do you put me through the trials of life?
Why is there so much pain in my heart?
Why do I have to struggle so much?
A gentle touch and I see a butterfly ascending to the sky,
And realization dawns, and all else fades away.
Why do I question and not trust thee?
Like the Butterfly, when my soul is ready to join thee,
I know you will release me from the clutches of this life,
Cleaning and polishing my soul to perfection,
And then, take me into Thine tender care and merge my soul into Thee.

Rest My Head In Your Lap

An incessant urge that we live with,
That freezes our thoughts rendering us useless,
Today I have thawed my life out of their clutches,
Releasing myself to realize the more celestial,
Rising above the mundane realities of life.

The truth, though staring at us all the time,
Is a silent spectator to our life passing by,
Ready to embrace us when we are ready,
Prodding us with its invisible tentacles,
Awakening us to meet our destiny.

What then binds us and doesn't let us let go?
What then stops us from practising what we know?
Hidden behind this facade of happiness lurks an
unsatisfied heart,
What stops me from breaking the thread and setting
myself free,
To find my way to rest my head in Your lap?

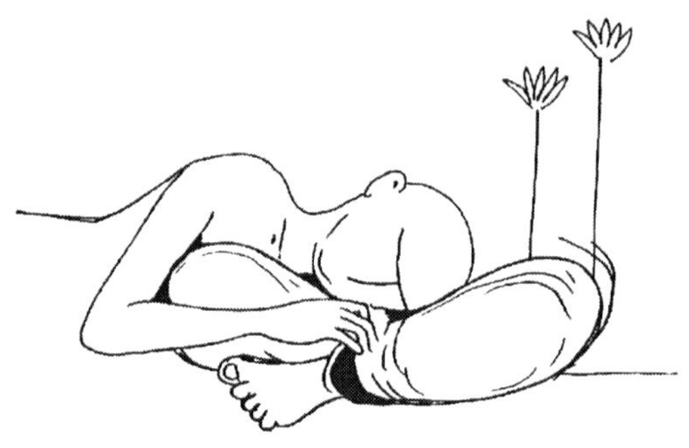

Krishna

Silently he walked
into my barren life,

Playing his
mystical flute,

A hypnotized me
walked blissfully,

Colouring my life
with his peacock feather,

Adorning and gracing my life with his presence,

He walked into my soul.

Our paths crossed umpteen times,

As he teasingly beckoned me,

Waiting for a right time that doesn't come,

I finally visited him with a soulmate.

Behold, there he stood in all majesty.

A grandeur that blessed the eye.

Mesmerizing me with his mischievous smile.

I closed my eyes, and my heart opened,

A thousand temple bells ringing kissed my ears.

The brightest of the rays enriched my senses ,

And a calm like none I know, spread across my being.

Were the pillars of his palace gold?

Floating lamps in the air.

Was it the green Tulsi mala or an offering of emerald?

The yellow marigold paled in comparison to him,

The blessed Kalinga, under his anklet, adorned tiny feet,
The dance of life and death, he seemed to say,

Am I not all-encompassed?

String Of My Soul

In this quiet land of a foreign motherland,
Surrounded by calm hills and moody mountains,
Trying to create our space and a place called home,
Strangers everywhere me to myself, as much as they to me.
Diving deep within, I know not who I am,
In this cemetery silence, I know nothing matters,
Life as well as death, Illusions or just a mirage urging us to go on,
Relatives and friends I reach out to,
My hands return empty.
No one to hold on to,
In this moment of despair, I look up,
And behold, oh Sai, there you are,
Holding the string of this beautiful soul in the hollow of this body,
Both, not my own.
I lay them before you, my lord
For you, at your leisure, to merge me into you.

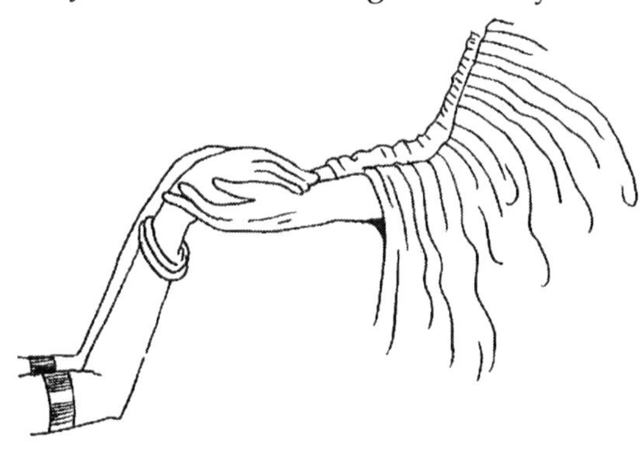

LOVE

"Love gives naught but itself and takes naught but from itself, Love possesses not nor would it be possessed: For love is sufficient unto love."

- Khalil Gibran, The Prophet.

Togetherness

A tiny thought that travels the entire universe,
Gathering all the happiness in the world for me.
A gentle whiff of the wind takes the pain and sorrow
away,
Before I see it, it is gone.

A silent murmur of unsung melodies of love flows into my
life,
Taking the unborn sigh away from my being.
A touch so gentle that brings every nerve to life,
A sight so majestic, the grandeur of it blinds my eye.

A thought so beautiful that blossoms into a smile,
A man so genuine that reinforces my belief in God.
Hushed footsteps enter my life,
Unspoken feelings surface to the brim.

Wordless emotions, the heart begins to spin,
Whispered words, a tranquil life begins to sing.
Who art thou? I try to question.
Will the answer make a difference, I ask?

A merciful angel's boon or a gift from a gracious god,
A sigh of relief in my morose life.
Or sunshine in my gloomy world,
Answers are long forgotten amidst the celebration.
Rejoicing in our togetherness, do I see you apart from
myself?

My Sunshine

Little raindrops fall gently on my face,
Awakening me and bringing me to my reality.
Soothing rays of the sun warm my soul,
And bring back to life what already was dead.

Do we know the impact we make on the life of others,
Are we aware of whose life we touch and make a difference.
Yet we go on living life on our own terms and conditions,
There you stand among your friends.

Unaware that a life you have changed,
A smile you bring to my lips.
A twinkle to my eye,
A song to my ears,
And a dream to my mind.

A lilt in my steps,
A joyous music in my heart.
A shiver in my senses,
And a tremble in my limbs.

Am I in love?
What is this blissful state that I am in?
Whatever it is, I do not wish to know.
Hoping this feeling never ends,

Hoping my love is eternally sealed.
Expectations none do I have,
At a distance, I want to stand and rejoice.
And live my life in this moment,
In this time.

Let Me Live

Like entering the sanctum of a temple,
A feeling of reverence spreads across my whole being.
When in your presence, I stand
My eyes look down, and my head bows.

You make me realize that my love is divine,
And the laws of the land do not bind me to them.
When you smile at me,
A mere mortal with its limitation, am I.

Yet you make me rise above the rest,
Evoking unconditional love.
Evolving me and carving me to be a better person,
Laugh you, might at my thoughts.

Yet unknowingly, you have given me the world,
A heart has learnt to love, a hand that has learnt to give.
And a body that has learnt to respond and revel,
In a world of your own, you live.

Where even my shadow has no place to bloom,
In a hope, I live that someday maybe.
A minuscule part of your life, I become
Do not want to elevate you to the position of the divine.

Yet to me, you are no less
I worship the ground you walk on and hold on to your words.
A madwoman, you might call me
I am unmoved by the names the world gives me.

Because my love for you surpasses all else that I know,
In a dreamlike state, I live
Not realizing when the day rolls into night,
Your thoughts occupy every corner of my mind.

Your face fills my eye.
In a blissful state, I live, caring a damn for the world.
Let me love you; let me live,
Do not ever take this right away from me.

Because then you might be walking over a corpse,
And that corpse would be mine.

Do Not Want To Hope

Do not want to hope
Do not want to dream.
I have heard the heartbreak
And it is not a pleasant sound.

I have heard teardrops echo in silent rooms
I have felt empty spaces sigh in grief.
I have tried to collect fragments of my broken relationships
An attempt so futile, I assure you.

Painful is but a frivolous word to describe this feeling
Hands that tremble to hold onto memories.
A mind that wants to let go but doesn't know how to
A heart that secretly beats with the name.

An eye that constantly searches for a glimpse of you
An ear that eagerly awaits to hear your voice.
A being that wants to be around you
And share the same earth and air.

A futile attempt to revive what exists no more
An attempt to hold and never let go.
A sinking feeling stops me from taking the hand extended
The hand of an unknown stranger.

Because I am me, only because of you
There is no space or need for anybody.
I am a complete person, and your thoughts make me so
Just need you to know.

That now, I do not want to hope
I do not want to dream.

Destiny Together

Like a sunflower that turns and
blooms in full,
Like a lotus that unfurls,
Like a pearl that takes birth,
Out of the ordinary, a mystery
unveils.

Reasons unknown yet insignificant,
A pilgrimage yet the destiny unknown,
A mist covers the path, yet my steps are firm,
For I know at each corner stand thou.

I look at you from a distance,
I know we have met in another place and time,
I know thee to be my soul mate,
A smile flowers as we make eye contact.

Do you feel the same?
Why that look in your eye, I ask?
No answers do I find, nor do I need any,
A silent agreement that none understand.

A mutual consent to wait for another time and place,
To be one again that none can separate,
Because we are on a mysterious path called life,
Duties to be fulfilled and needs to be met.

Before we, on our personal journeys, embark,
Yet I know at some crossroads I will find you again.
With extended arms and love in your eyes,
Waiting to fulfil our destiny together.

You Are Not There

A sinking feeling envelopes my heart.
As I know the excitement this day brings into your life,
A new beginning for you,
And an end to mine.

Like a lost child, I wander aimlessly, Can't feel a thing,
Distant voices call me, but I can't hear, I walk on.

I turn back to see,
But you are not there,
My eyes search as I run wildly to all our favourite haunts,
You are not there; you are not here.

Why do things change?
Tears flow; they don't listen to me,
A feeling so numb slowly spreads,
A corpse lies here now, waiting for the vultures to devour.

Forever Is A Convenient Word

The breeze carries your song into a stranger's ears,
Your caring hands now guide another,
Your loving glances have changed directions,
Your eye doesn't recognize me,
Nor do your lips respond to mine.

Forever is a convenient word.
Lasts a lifetime,
Or maybe a year or some,
Forever alas, does not last forever,
Reasons are trivial and futile.

What is lost can never be found again,
Days that were so never will be again.
The water is seeping in through cracks,
Strangers in the garb of friends,
Trying to go on as if nothing happened.

Except a year lost in the paradise
of love.
The slightest hint creates ripples
of uneasiness,
And the silence and oblivion.

Where Do I Seek Solace?

Where do I seek solace?
Who will comfort me,
Who will love me like you did,
Unconditional and selfless?

The voices echo in the hallways of my memories,
Pictures of our love adorn the walls,
Captured but never to breathe again,
Each word strung into beautiful songs.

That will never be sung again.
Each hug and touch frozen in time,
The memories of which give me warmth,
Each memory decorates the barren land of my heart.

Where nothing will grow ever again, Come summer,
winter, and spring, Nothing will sprout again.

Seasons Change

Seasons change, but feelings don't,
Spring is here with fresh blossoms,
The Chinar leaves have stopped falling,
As have the snowflakes.

Seasons change as our relationships,
Time moves on; nothing is constant,
Nothing except the emptiness of a hollow existence,
The sun glares, and I have nobody to hide behind.

The weights I carry, nobody to unburden me,
The tears that I shed, nobody to wipe them,
Time moves on; nothing is constant,
Except the emptiness.

Change is constant, cannot keep pace.
In some forsaken forbidden land, I find myself,
Where the chains of memories bind me, a prisoner for life,
Hallucinating a happy life together.

For You, I Pray?

For you, I pray,
Let the sun always
shine on thy dwelling,
And the gentle shower
brings thy comfort,
Let the pleasant breeze carry fragrance to thy beloved,
And may you rejoice in your union.

For you, I pray,
For thee who was my almighty,
Whom I worshipped and loved,
For you who taught me to love again.

Whom I treasure and will love till I die,
For you, I pray.

Let your thoughts and wishes transform into realities,
Where nothing is too great to achieve,
Let all your dreams spring to life,
Where nothing is impossible, and everything is in your
reach.

For you, I pray,
For you, as for myself,
Because your happiness brings me the greatest joy,
Because your grief breaks me each time and renders me
helpless,
For thee, I pray who is my soul mate, though I may not be
yours.

Another Age And Time

Drops of tears string into beautiful pearls,
A wave of sighs gathers to form the breeze.
A flood of words and emotions woven into a poem,
Pieces of a broken heart take to wings like a bird.

Destiny has played its game,
Few have won, and the rest have lost.
But life is life; it moves on,
A flickering candle in the storm.

The soul has lived through its many trials,
Soulmates have failed to endure the relationships.
Just happy being mates, they move on,
Leaving an unfinished story for another age and time.

Like A Falling Star

Like a falling star, I fell into the unknown abyss,
Like innumerable little may flowers, I was crushed,
Like the unwanted wind, I was shut out,
A feeling so numb spreads like slow poison.

Until I feel no pain, grief or hatred,
A feeling so disoriented,
Lost and lonely, I walk on,
Into the dark dungeons of life.

Shrieks of false laughter and fake smiles,
The noise of meaningless empty words,
Unfinished Stories of untrue love,
Fills surrounds and strangles me.

Where do I run? How do I live?
The thread that binds us is so delicate and thin,
A pull and we come apart in heart, mind and soul,
Strangers in seconds.

Death of Love

The brightest of days change into the darkest of nights,
The masks cannot be adorned for long,
The pretense cannot hide the real self,
The face is hideously scary and unnerving,
It takes a microsecond to forget and move on,
Love and respect shattered and scattered underfoot,
He walks on,
Towards greener pastures to step ahead in life,
Without looking back to see the death of love.

A Silent End

A silent end to a beautiful dream,
No justification, no ugly scenes, no farewell.
Just a silent end to a beautiful dream,
A quiet nudge and I wake up to face reality.
Refreshed and rejuvenated by a long sleep,
I walk on.
A silent end to a beautiful dream,
Things that I had always longed for.
Came alive in all splendour and brought me to life,
A dream that taught me to live again.
Feelings long forgotten, sensations lost,
Tracked their way into my being.
Smiles flowered, my heart bloomed,
I felt a sense of grandeur from inside, worthy of the priceless, I lived like there was no tomorrow,
And I realize now that there is no tomorrow.
Because it is a silent end to a beautiful dream.

Darkness

Darkness spreads all around,
Silence rules the surroundings.
My heart numb feels no pain or happiness,
No wishes or desires survive the trials.
A gentle breeze slowly uncovers the dark veils,
A tiny ray of light seeps in,
Threatens to flicker and vanishes,
Holding on to a word of love,
I hang on for dear life.
Uncertainty rules at large,
To fit into your life,
To be loved is a heavy price to pay,
Individuality lost.
Slaughtered and slain lies the real me,
No man loves another more than himself,
A sad smile touches my lips.
I realize the darkness and silence are my friends,
At least they let me be me.

With The Fall Of The Chinar Leaves

With the fall of the Chinar leaves,
You brought a ray of fresh sunshine,
Into the dark vacuum of my life,
You taught me to live again.

With every drop of a snowflake,
You reached out and touched my soul,
Lost and dead, you brought it to life again,
And gave meaning to my life.

With the very look of your eye,
You stirred my soul and opened a thousand doors,
And made me
realize,
We were meant to
be one.

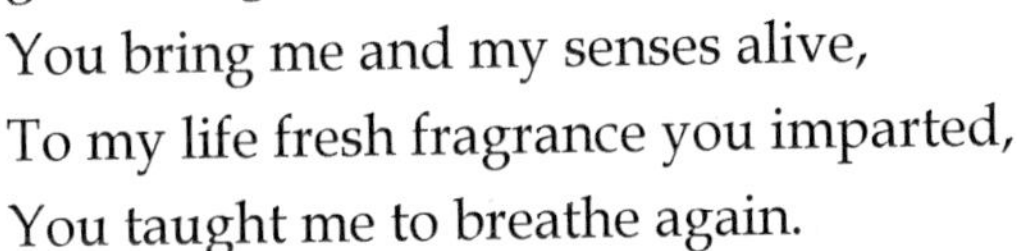

With the tender
touch of your
gentle fingers,
You bring me and my senses alive,
To my life fresh fragrance you imparted,
You taught me to breathe again.

With your presence in my life,
You made me realize that I am a person too,
Your love and respect have me indebted to you,
Not only in this lifetime but the next one too.

Standing At A Distance

Standing at a distance, Young and confused,
Unable to put my feelings into words,
I saw you surrounded by impenetrable walls.

To pierce it, of humiliation and rejection,
I saw no strength but only desires rise,
Desires that couldn't stand the test of time,
For no hint of your feelings reached me.

Until I was totally submerged,
Drowned and gasping for breath,
Today I see my future surrounded by walls of uncertainty,
Today the meaning of my entire life has changed.

The tides of life have won, And I am tired to fight it.
Yet each year, I await your return, To be alive again,
If only in dreams and moments spent with you.

A Word Called Life

On a cold dark night,
A thought like a glow-worm
glows,
A memory kindles my soul,
gives it warmth,
A smile lands on my lips.

Though we walk on
different paths,
Our roads often cross,
A stolen hug, a heartfelt
word, and a glance in
eternity,
Makes my life a worthwhile
one.

No tears do I shed anymore for things that could have
been,
For I know that though knots do not bind us together,
It is our hearts that often touch and bond,
To bring freshness and excitement to our life.

Relationships cannot always be defined,
It is for us to live and know,
To experience the difference,
And to love a word called Life.

Forgive Me

Forgive me, my friend,
For my life is not my own.
It is twisted and knotted with other lives too,
The wind of freedom blows every now and then.
Only to be anchored by them,
Into a dozen roles, I mould myself each day.
Unsatisfied souls, I leave at each junction,
Their thirst I cannot quench.
My soul and body are squeezed to the maximum,
What else is left to be offered?
On each altar, sacrificed each day in a thousand-one ways,
I arise only stronger than before,
Like the phoenix, I have no death,
Eternally bond to the land of pain and sorrow.
A breath of fresh air you bring into my life,
Yet time and again, I take you to the eternal hell of dissatisfaction,
Of a life of incomplete happiness and empty companionship,
I have offered you my soul and my heart.
But vultures and scavengers are waiting to tear my body apart,
Please forgive me that forever I ask for your understanding,
My love can only beg of thee, for they are all deaf-eared.

Loneliness Has A New Address

In search of love,
In pursuit of happiness,
Life seems to pass by,
Loneliness has a new address and meaning.

Reduced to a body that walks in the crowd,
Without a name or an identity,
Blind and deaf to the world,
It walks on, a vacuum in its heart and being.

Emptiness so massive that the laughter of the entire world
cannot fill,
Where every sigh is measured against the other,
And the prize is a hollow of a body that aimlessly walks
by,
On roads that remain untrodden and unheard of.

Thoughts and feelings that you do not want to
acknowledge,
They exist and will survive the days and nights,
A telephone number that can be barred,
A nameless existence in your gadgets and life.

Taking the form of words in my poetry,
Or the shape of tears in my dewy eyes,
You live in me as my breath and my laughter,
In an unperceivable existence, the woman that I am.

Reach Out

A sudden rush of events, Confusion at its peak,
Voices at their highest pitches,
Senseless talks and emotionless feelings,
Leave me alone. . .
I don't want to belong,
Belong to your mundane life throbbing with baseless issues,
Ready to burst with the slightest of pressure. . .
Leave me alone. . .
I don't belong to your land or your ways.
Look into my eyes and speak.
My soul wants to talk to yours,
Feel me with your eyes and not your skin,
Listen to what my breath says. . .
Does your breath sing the same song as mine?
When was the last time you tasted a raindrop?
Do you also feel intoxicated by it?
Come with me and live again.
Rejoice in the gift of life and bask in life's little joys,
Reach out and hold my extended hand,
If you pause to think, Behold.
Into thin air, I will just merge,
Merge, and you will never find me again.
Just my fragrant memory will linger on for a while,
Then the chaos will envelop you and,
I will be just another casually tossed thought.

A thought that you will gladly part;
To live your Life. Your way.

Love

When I hear the crushing sound of tiny thudding bits of
my heart,
I promise myself; never again will I fall in love,
Many a promise has been broken to be made again,
Yet each time, I live with hope and give myself another
chance.
I turn back and see the faces of people, whom I have loved,
And I slowly see their images fading away,
Fading away, as their shortcoming which I chose to ignore,
Love doesn't blind, yet it teaches you to ignore. . .
It teaches you to accept until it threatens your existence.

My Naked Face

Far away into the valley I wish to walk,
No footsteps do I want to leave behind,
Lest anybody follows me and see the flood of emotions raising
Curbed and hidden behind a thousand smiles.
Where did I go wrong or was I never on the right track?
My heart churns and a cry so helpless springs out,
Surprising my controlled senses,
My naked face evident to all.

Acknowledgements

My deepest thanks to Vandana Bhatia Palli - Founder, Highbrow Scribes Publications, Lalitha Ravindran - First Forays Literary Agency, for your Guidance and Support.

Rohit Bhasi - for the Cover and Illustrations.

Nandita Chakraborty – author / friend for your encouragement.

My family and friends for your belief in me.

My Guru and Ishta Devatas for your blessings.